Social Media

Connect with a community of *Bible Studies for Life* users. Post responses to questions, share teaching ideas, and link to great blog content. **Facebook.com/BibleStudiesForLife**

Get instant updates about new articles, giveaways, and more. **@BibleMeetsLife**

The App

Simple and straightforward, this elegantly designed iPhone app gives you all the content of the Small Group Member Book—plus a whole lot more—right at your fingertips. Available in the iTunes App Store; search **"Bible Studies for Life."**

Blog

At **BibleStudiesForLife.com/blog** you will find all the magazine articles we mention in this study guide and music downloads provided by LifeWay Worship. Plus, leaders and group members alike will benefit from the blog posts written for people in every life stage—singles, parents, boomers, and senior adults—as well as media clips, connections between our study topics, current events, and much more.

Training

For helps on how to use Bible Studies for Life, tips on how to better lead groups, or additional ideas for leading this session, visit: **www.ministrygrid.com/web/biblestudiesforlife.**

Ready: Ministering Life to Those in Crisis
Bible Studies for Life: Small Group Member Book

© 2014 LifeWay Press

ISBN: 978-1-4300-3500-8

Item: 005680982

Dewey Decimal Classification Number: 259

Subject Heading: LAY MINISTRY \ LOVE \ HELPING BEHAVIOR

Eric Geiger
Vice President, Church Resources

Ronnie Floyd
General Editor

David Francis
Managing Editor

Gena Rogers
Sam O'Neal
Content Editors

Philip Nation
Director, Adult Ministry Publishing

Faith Whatley
Director, Adult Ministry

Send questions/comments to: Content Editor, *Bible Studies for Life: Adults*, One LifeWay Plaza, Nashville, TN 37234-0175; or make comments on the Web at *www.BibleStudiesforLife.com*

Printed in the United States of America

For ordering or inquiries, visit www.lifeway.com; write LifeWay Small Groups; One LifeWay Plaza; Nashville, TN 37234-0152; or call toll free (800) 458-2772.

All Scripture quotations, unless otherwise indicated, are taken from the Holman Christian Standard Bible®, copyright 1999, 2000, 2002, 2003, 2009 by Holman Bible Publishers. Used by permission.

Bible Studies for Life: Adults often lists websites that may be helpful to our readers. Our staff verifies each site's usefulness and appropriateness prior to publication. However, website content changes quickly so we encourage you to approach all websites with caution. Make sure sites are still appropriate before sharing them with students, friends, and family.

D1223665

You're called to minister. Be ready.

Charles Dickens wrote, "It was the best of times, it was the worst of times," as the first line of his famous novel *A Tale of Two Cities*. I'm reminded of that opening because we may well be living in "the worst of times" today. Many in our culture have rejected absolute truth, the values in society are shifting, and the moral foundation of our nation is crumbling before our eyes. It's easy to feel discouraged. And it's tempting to insulate ourselves from the messiness of a culture that's far from God.

But this may also be the best of times. Why? Because the opportunity for ministry has never been greater. God didn't call us to retreat or run for the hills. He called us to be "in the world" (John 17:11-19) and to be "the light" of the gospel (Matt. 5:14-16) in a dark and broken society.

That's why I've created this study. In order for us to be ready to minister, we must be on the alert.

Specifically, this study will help you be more sensitive to some of the struggles and addictions that people in your community are facing. This study will also give you a biblical understanding and perspective for ministering in the midst of those crises.

Every struggle, addiction, and sin involves and affects a person who has been created in the image of God. It's not enough to have minds equipped with truth; we must also have hearts moved with compassion. This study will give you practical ways to love, support, and minister to those in crisis.

In the pages ahead, we're going to tackle some of the most challenging issues of our day. If you will engage these sessions, you will be ready to minister when someone considers an abortion, when those around you experience poverty, when sickness comes to stay, when sex threatens to destroy, when families are torn apart by homosexuality, and when someone is trapped by pornography.

Chip Ingram

Chip Ingram serves as senior pastor of Venture Christian Church in Los Gatos, California, and as teaching pastor of Living on the Edge, an international teaching and discipleship ministry. He is the author of 12 books, including one that tackles many of the issues addressed in this study: *Culture Shock: A Biblical Response to Today's Most Divisive Issues* (Baker Books).

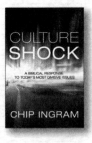

contents

SESSION 1

READY WHEN INJUSTICE PREVAILS

What examples of injustice cause your blood to boil?

QUESTION #1

#BSFLinjustice

> *God calls us to defend those who can't defend themselves.*

THE BIBLE MEETS LIFE

Every few years, a trial takes place that captures the nation's attention. The case may involve a celebrity or some sensational murder, and it seems to be the only thing the national media talks about. And when the jury finally reaches a verdict, we hear a collective cry of surprise at their decision: not guilty!

"How could they let that person go free when all the evidence and testimony pointed to their guilt? They got away with murder!"

We've all had those moments when we marveled at a blatant lack of justice. But many examples of injustice go unnoticed: negligence, abuse, oppression, murder—the list goes on. Injustice often hits hardest against those who are unable to speak up for themselves. Who sees that justice is done for those without a voice?

God is a God of justice and He calls us, His people, to practice justice. In the Old Testament, we see clear-cut direction on how we should practice justice and speak up for others. Rather than letting our blood boil over injustice, we can step in and be a voice for the voiceless.

WHAT DOES THE BIBLE SAY?

Exodus 23:1-3,6-9 (HCSB)

1 "You must not spread a false report. Do not join the wicked to be a malicious witness.

2 "You must not follow a crowd in wrongdoing. Do not testify in a lawsuit and go along with a crowd to pervert justice.

3 Do not show favoritism to a poor person in his lawsuit. "

6 "You must not deny justice to a poor person among you in his lawsuit.

7 Stay far away from a false accusation. Do not kill the innocent and the just, because I will not justify the guilty.

8 "You must not take a bribe, for a bribe blinds the clear-sighted and corrupts the words of the righteous.

9 You must not oppress a foreign resident; you yourselves know how it feels to be a foreigner because you were foreigners in the land of Egypt."

Key Words

The innocent (v. 7)—The Hebrew describes a person generally characterized as godly or righteous. In this passage the word refers to a person who has committed no crime and deserves no punishment.

Oppress (v. 9)—The Hebrew literally means "to squeeze." Its common use in the Old Testament refers to cruel treatment. The Israelites were "squeezed" in Egypt but commanded not to "squeeze" others.

Exodus 23:1-3

Justice is an ideal in every society. And one way to carry out justice is to fight against the corrosion of lies and deceit. That's the focus of the commands recorded in Exodus 23:1-3.

Specifically, we're commanded not to "spread a false report." I can't read these verses without thinking about justice for the unborn children of our world. Why? Because one false report that has circulated for years is the claim that an unborn child is only "tissue" or a "product of conception." Abortion isn't an ethical or moral issue, the argument goes, because it doesn't involve "real" human beings.

Advancements in technology have shed light on this false report. Today we have access to 4-D ultrasounds, which is great because 85 percent of women who benefit from this technology decide to keep their babies—it's clear that what's inside the womb is a human life.

▶ The heart begins to beat between the 18th and 24th day after conception.

▶ Brain waves have been recorded as early as 45 days after conception.

▶ At eight weeks, the baby possesses the unique fingerprints he or she will have for life.

▶ At 11-12 weeks, a baby can suck its thumb.[1]

Given these truths, why have so many embraced a "false report" about abortion? Because the lie protects them from unwanted consequences and responsibility. Injustice occurs when people are willing to seek their freedom at the expense of someone else's life.

It's easy to go along with the culture on controversial issues. But God's command is clear: "You must not follow a crowd in wrongdoing" (v. 2). Our call is equally clear: stand up for others who can't stand up for themselves. Don't join in the falsehoods and lies against them.

Why are we sometimes tempted to blend in with the crowd?

QUESTION #2

Exodus 23:6-7

Let me state the obvious: it is a great injustice—a sin, in fact—to kill anyone. People have tried to justify euthanasia or the taking of any life they deem non-viable or unproductive, but Scripture doesn't give us that option. **The Bible upholds the sanctity of human life.**

Now, most people read these verses with a sigh of relief. We think: "I haven't killed anyone. Whew!" But we also need to consider whether we're contributing to murder through inaction. Look at the full context of this passage. The law addressed the issue of seeing justice universally carried out. We aren't to favor the poor person in a matter (v. 3), but neither are we to deny him justice. A lack of justice can lead to an innocent person's wrongful death. And our inaction—our failure to prevent an injustice—can be equally harmful.

I realize abortion isn't a topic for casual discussion; your group would probably prefer to talk about something else. But there are lives at stake. This isn't simply a theological or theoretical issue. This issue impacts family members, neighbors, friends, coworkers, and your church. Here are the facts:

> More than one out of every five pregnancies ends in abortion.

> Sixty-five percent of all women who have abortions identify themselves as Christians.

> Since Roe v. Wade in 1973, more than 56 million babies have been killed in the U. S. through abortion.[2] (For some context, the total population of California is around 40 million.)

What's more, every abortion sets off a chain reaction of loss. Parents are impacted. Untold numbers of people deal with the guilt of knowing they participated in or supported an abortion. All these repercussions are sobering, and the gravity of the situation is magnified when we consider God's response: "I will not justify the guilty" (v. 7). Those who contribute to the death of an innocent person become guilty themselves because of their unjust actions. God takes sin and injustice seriously.

> *How does this passage influence your response to issues such as abortion?*
>
> QUESTION #3

Exodus 23:8-9

One group that is susceptible to oppression and unfair treatment in any culture is the outsider—those who are "not like us." God gave the Israelites a strong reason for treating foreigners with fairness: they had been outsiders themselves. The Israelites had been oppressed and unfairly treated in Egypt; therefore, God called them to remember their own experiences. Implicit in this command is the heart of the Golden Rule: treat others as you want to be treated.

We place value on the object by virtue of who created it. (Try purchasing a painting by Van Gogh or Picasso for the same price as a painting by a talented, but unknown artist.) In Genesis 1:27 we read, "So God created man in His own image; He created him in the image of God." God took His stamp, His image, and implanted it on every human being on this planet. That gives each human being infinite value and worth.

What's more, we never lose our value in God's eyes. Even when our lives are full of sin, even when we've been guilty of oppressing others, He steps in and removes our guilt when we repent. Because God is holy, He will not justify or ignore our guilt. But Jesus— the One with no sin or guilt—took our sin and guilt upon Himself. He removes our sin and offers us forgiveness in Christ.

We can and should apply that same value to others. We do just that when we work tirelessly to stop the great injustice of abortion. We do that when we help those struggling under the guilt of abortion see that God's grace is available for them. We do that when we treat all people fairly and work for the justice of others. We do that when we do all we can to see that the innocent and the oppressed are shown the respect and value God gives them.

Most of all, we treat others with the value they deserve when we point them to the freedom we all need in Christ.

> *How does justice in this passage compare with the "justice" we typically see?*
>
> **QUESTION #4**

> *What behaviors can we adopt or change in order to defend those who can't defend themselves?*
>
> **QUESTION #5**

FINDING VALUE

Write a sentence under each of the following images explaining why the object it represents should be considered valuable.

What prevents us from always treating people the way God sees and values them?

Your eyes saw me when I was formless—all my days were written in your book and planned before a single one of them began."

—PSALM 139:16

LIVE IT OUT

Consider what you can do this week to address the pain of wrong decisions and defend the lives of others:

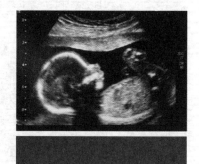

▶ **Pray.** Pray each day for the thousands of unborn babies currently at risk. Pray for the women and families that have been impacted by abortion.

▶ **Get involved.** Consider writing letters to your congressional representative and other elected officials on this vital issue.

▶ **Give what you can.** Contribute to a local crisis-pregnancy center. Donate money or volunteer your time to help in this important work.

Abortion is not the "unpardonable sin." God can bring beauty from ashes and healing from the pain of wrong decisions—and from the pain of failing to prevent wrong decisions. God values us. He values others. So let's follow suit and do the same.

Excerpt: Orphan Justice

"Johnny, what would have happened to your little girl if she hadn't been adopted?"

My friend Matt's words cut through the cool night air as we leaned against his pickup truck while watching our sons' baseball practice. Xiaoli came running by, laughing with glee as she dodged behind me to avoid getting tagged, then bolted off across the parking lot.

To continue reading this excerpt from *Orphan Justice*, by Johnny Carr, visit *BibleStudiesforLife.com/articles*.

My group's prayer requests

....

....

....

....

....

....

....

....

....

....

My thoughts

1. "Pro-Life America," [cited 8 May 2014]. Available from the Internet: *www.prolife.com.*; "Medline Plus–Fetal Development," [cited 8 May 2014]. Available from the Internet: *www.nlm.nih.gov.*
2. "Induced Abortion in the United States," Guttmacher Institute, February 2014 [cited 16 April 2014]. Available from the Internet: *www.guttmacher.org.*

SESSION 2

READY TO HELP THE POOR

What would you have a hard time living without?

#BSFLpoor

Demonstrate God's heart for the poor.

THE BIBLE MEETS LIFE

Several years ago I realized I'd been reading the Bible with blinders on. Somehow I'd skipped right over the many passages that deal with the poor.

I've always given my tithe to my local church, and I've been on a journey for the last 25 years to give proportionally above that. I felt like I was doing great—until I was challenged to read the Bible with fresh eyes and look for all the commands and references to the poor, the orphan, and the widow.

Somewhere along the line my heart had become insensitive. Giving a few dollars to individuals or through my church became a substitute for true generosity. In the words of Deuteronomy 15, I was "hardhearted" and "tightfisted."

Thankfully, this passage in Deuteronomy also shows me the other side: the blessing of being generous to those in need. Let's consider how we can help others in need—and in the process demonstrate the very heart of God.

WHAT DOES THE BIBLE SAY?

Deuteronomy 15:7-11 *(HCSB)*

7 "If there is a poor person among you, one of your brothers within any of your gates in the land the LORD your God is giving you, you must not be hardhearted or tightfisted toward your poor brother.

8 Instead, you are to open your hand to him and freely loan him enough for whatever need he has.

9 Be careful that there isn't this wicked thought in your heart, 'The seventh year, the year of canceling debts, is near,' and you are stingy toward your poor brother and give him nothing. He will cry out to the LORD against you, and you will be guilty.

10 Give to him, and don't have a stingy heart when you give, and because of this the LORD your God will bless you in all your work and in everything you do.

11 For there will never cease to be poor people in the land; that is why I am commanding you, 'You must willingly open your hand to your afflicted and poor brother in your land.'"

Key Words

The year of canceling debts (v. 9)—God commanded Israel to let their fields lie fallow every seven years (Ex. 23:10-11; Lev. 25:1-7). Deuteronomy 15 added the command to forgive debts of fellow Israelites on those occasions.

Bless (v. 10)—The Hebrew refers to divine favor bestowed on a person for righteous behavior. In Deuteronomy 15:10, God promised blessings upon the person who gave generously to the needy.

Deuteronomy 15:7-9

As God convicted my heart and I began to read Scripture with fresh eyes, whole sections of the Bible came alive for me. In particular, God's concern for orphans struck a chord. My family had supported orphans through some good ministries, but to be honest, we did so in order to "teach" our kids about helping others. Beyond that, orphans were definitely not on my heart or reflected in my finances.

But before I share the amazing adventure God has taken me on, let's look a little more closely at God's instruction to the Israelites as they prepared to enter the promised land. The core principles God taught His people in those days will also help us live generously and give generously according to His will.

> *What do you think of when you hear the word "generosity"?*
>
> QUESTION #2

The command in verses 7-8 is pretty straightforward: "If there is a poor person among you, one of your brothers within any of your gates in the land the LORD your God is giving you, you must not be hardhearted or tightfisted toward your poor brother. Instead, you are to open your hand to him and freely loan him enough for whatever need he has."

When it comes to living generously toward the poor, Moses pointed out the two biggest truths:

1. Generosity is a heart issue.

2. Generosity is a hand issue.

The heart has everything to do with attitude, and the hand has everything to do with action. The heart is about belief, and the hand is about behavior.

> *How is generosity toward the poor both a heart issue and a hand issue?*
>
> QUESTION #3

Earlier in Deuteronomy 15, Moses introduced a new command related to the sabbatical year: every seven years the Israelites were to cancel all debts. Sometimes people view the Old Testament as a collection of harsh rules and stories, but Deuteronomy 15 is a great example of God's grace, mercy, and kindness. If God's people would obey His commands concerning lending and borrowing—including collecting, repaying, and forgiving debts—the Lord assured them "there will be no poor among you" (v. 4). What an amazing promise!

Unfortunately, people often have trouble following God's commands. Because God knew that, He gave a stern warning in verse 9: "Be careful that there isn't this wicked thought in your heart, 'The seventh year, the year of canceling debts, is near,' and you are stingy toward your poor brother and give him nothing. He will cry out to the LORD against you, and you will be guilty."

It might be easy for us to judge the Israelites and wonder: *How could they be so uncaring toward their fellow people?* But how many times do we rationalize and find excuses for not being generous toward the poor in our own communities?

Deuteronomy 15:10-11

The appeal to both "heart" and "hand" continues in verses 10-11. Look at verse 10, for example: "Give to him, and don't have a stingy heart when you give, and because of this the Lord your God will bless you in all your work and in everything you do." Know this: God is always interested in your "heart" as much as your "hand." He wants you to live generously, but He also wants you to do so for the right reasons.

HEART AND HAND

HEART	HAND
Below are several practical consequences of poverty around the world. Circle the consequences that most arouse your compassion or make your blood boil.	What's one action you can take to begin combatting these consequences in your community through the practice of generosity?

HUNGER   HOMELESSNESS

HUMAN TRAFFICKING

ILLITERACY   CHILD LABOR

MALNUTRITION   CRIME

DISEASE   ADDICTION

DRUG TRAFFICKING

CHILD ABUSE   ORPHANS

"In the Scriptures, no national crime is condemned so frequently, and few so strongly, as oppression and cruelty."

—WILLIAM WILBERFORCE

Notice that God didn't call Israel to do the bare minimum. He didn't tell them to just meet the need or give the least amount they could afford. He called the Israelites to a high standard of generosity. This principle should be even more tangible and powerful for us who follow Christ. **We have personally experienced God's generosity toward us in the coming of Jesus; therefore, we should express generosity to others.**

These truths are repeated throughout the Bible. For example, James 5:1-6 gives a strong warning to those of us who are rich (like many of us who are Americans). God is not opposed to wealth, but He is opposed to the misuse and abuse of wealth. That's why James exposed the shadowy side of wealth and rebuked it.

James also described critical ways we are to handle our wealth:

1. **Don't hoard your money.** James warned against hoarding wealth, money, and clothes. This is about what you do with the wealth you have accumulated.

2. **Don't waste your money.** James reprimanded those who live in luxury and self-indulgence. This is about how we spend the money we have. When we live indulgently, we are being excessive, wasteful, and self-gratifying.

3. **Be generous with your money.** The key antidote to hoarding and self-indulgent living is generosity. This is about how we use our resources to bless others and, thus, bring God's blessing into our lives. True fulfillment and joy come from giving.

I didn't solve my blindness concerning the poor by waiting until it went away and then becoming generous. Instead, the solution was for me to simply act on where I wanted my heart to be. I started giving what was for me a significant amount to orphans through a friend's ministry I knew well and trusted deeply. As I gave, I read the reports of how my giving was being used.

After a few years my wife, Theresa, and I went to Zimbabwe to visit the homes and orphans we had been supporting. We stood in amazement at how God used our gifts, money, and time to change lives—both spiritually and physically.

What factors should we consider when seeking to help the poor?

QUESTION **#4**

How does this passage challenge us to be fully engaged in ministry to the poor?

QUESTION **#5**

LIVE IT OUT

How will you change in light of these truths from God's Word? Consider these practical ideas for serving the poor:

▶ **Remove the blinders.** Make an effort in the coming days to seek out the poor and underprivileged in your community. Consider looking where you don't typically look and going where you don't typically go.

▶ **Plan to give.** Set up your budget to include a monthly amount for giving when you encounter spontaneous needs.

▶ **Get involved.** Find a local ministry your church supports that helps the poor, the orphans, or the needy. Choose to become an active contributor.

When my money and time were directed to the poor, my heart, attitude, and actions toward them changed as well. The same can be true of you. Let's lose those blind spots as the church!

Christ in a Coffee Shop

I called him Two-Phone Joe. The first time I met him, I was sitting at an outdoor table at my favorite coffee spot when he came out, cell phone pressed between shoulder and ear, talking a blue streak. He had a cup of coffee in one hand, a Coke in the other, and another phone on his belt. When he put his cup down to hang up, I said, "Man, you've got to relax a little!" And that's how my friendship got started with one of the most hyper guys I've ever known.

To continue reading "Christ in a Coffee Shop" from *Mature Living* magazine, visit *BibleStudiesforLife.com/articles*.

My group's prayer requests

My thoughts

SESSION 3

READY WHEN SICKNESS COMES TO STAY

When you're sick, what helps you feel better?

QUESTION #1

#BSFLgrace

God's grace is sufficient—even in times of sickness.

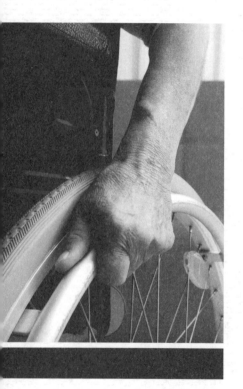

THE BIBLE MEETS LIFE

When I think about sickness, I remember my parents. My mom endured years of treatments for a rare blood disorder that ultimately destroyed her body and required amputation to prolong her life. My father went from a 75-year-old man riding in 100-mile bike treks with people half his age to a wheelchair in an assisted living center.

Both my parents died after long and painful journeys through sickness. Both were Christians who loved God. Both had seen God answer miraculous prayers in different seasons of their lives. Both had asked God for earthly healing in their own lives, yet both received "no" as God's answer in their final years.

Anyone who struggles with long-term health issues will come to this question sooner or later: If God can heal me, why doesn't He?

Some of the most profound teaching and insight on this issue came from the pen of the apostle Paul. He was a man well acquainted with pain and suffering throughout his life. He understood. So, let's look at an account from His life recorded in 2 Corinthians.

WHAT DOES THE BIBLE SAY?

2 Corinthians 4:16-18; 12:7b-10 (HCSB)

4:16 Therefore we do not give up. Even though our outer person is being destroyed, our inner person is being renewed day by day.

17 For our momentary light affliction is producing for us an absolutely incomparable eternal weight of glory.

18 So we do not focus on what is seen, but on what is unseen. For what is seen is temporary, but what is unseen is eternal.

12:7b Therefore, so that I would not exalt myself, a thorn in the flesh was given to me, a messenger of Satan to torment me so I would not exalt myself.

8 Concerning this, I pleaded with the Lord three times to take it away from me.

9 But He said to me, "My grace is sufficient for you, for power is perfected in weakness." Therefore, I will most gladly boast all the more about my weaknesses, so that Christ's power may reside in me.

10 So I take pleasure in weaknesses, insults, catastrophes, persecutions, and in pressures, because of Christ. For when I am weak, then I am strong.

Key Words

Grace (12:9)—The Greek term can also mean "mercy," "kindness," "goodwill," "gift," or "beauty." It is generally understood as God's undeserved favor.

Sufficient (12:9)—The word translated *sufficient* primarily means "to ward off," thus "to defend," "to be strong," or "to be enough."

Perfected (12:9)—As it is used in this context the verb means "made complete" or "made fully present."

2 Corinthians 4:16-18

In 2 Corinthians 4, Paul described his current situation with words like "pressured," "perplexed," "persecuted," "struck down," and "given over to death." Even though Paul's outward circumstances were extremely hard, he used very different words and phrases to describe his inward attitude: "not crushed," "not in despair," "not abandoned," and "not destroyed" (see verses 8-9).

What enabled Paul to have that kind of attitude? Verses 16-18 show us the answer: in spite of his earthly difficulties, Paul maintained an eternal perspective. "Therefore we do not give up," he wrote. "Even though our outer person is being destroyed, our inner person is being renewed day by day" (v. 16).

Such a viewpoint is rare in our culture. Today, a person's hope, happiness, and even identity are typically tied to his or her physical health or circumstances. Because Paul had an eternal perspective, however, he was able to be strong and joyful when most people would feel weak and depressed.

Imagine a set of scales. On one side of the scale, Paul gathered up all of his suffering and trials. On the other side was the eternal glory that would be his when he reached heaven with Jesus. Paul concluded that the coming eternal glory was far heavier—far greater—than the sufferings of his earthly life.

The same is true for us. When compared with the eternal glory that's been promised to us, the sufferings of this life are momentary—brief and fleeting. They are light and easy to bear.

Pain has a way of rocking our world in a good way; it can help us shift our focus. We realize we're mortal and won't be here forever. We come to see, as Scripture says, that this physical life is "like smoke that appears for a little while, then vanishes" (Jas. 4:14). **When life gets hard—even unbearable— the Lord encourages us to remember that we're not home yet.**

What are some questions people ask as they deal with health-related issues?

QUESTION **#2**

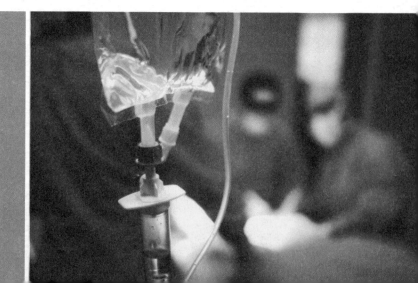

2 Corinthians 12:7b-9a

In 2 Corinthians 12, we see one very specific example from Paul's life about his own journey with suffering. We can read of Paul's request for relief and deliverance from his "thorn in the flesh." Bible scholars have conjectured as to what exactly was Paul's thorn in the flesh. No one can say with certainty what it was, but it was likely some kind of physical affliction.

Paul repeatedly petitioned God to remove his affliction. Repeatedly, however, God's answer was no. And as far as we know, God gave no explanation for refusing Paul.

That's an important lesson for us today. Implicit in God's "no" is the gentle challenge to "trust Me." Even when we don't understand His plan, we can still trust His character.

While God didn't remove the thorn that was oppressing Paul, He did make two promises to His servant:

1. **God's ever-present grace would be sufficient.**
   God didn't remove the thorn, but He did promise Paul He would provide everything the apostle needed to live with it. This reminds me of the psalmist's words in Psalm 34:18: "The Lord is near the brokenhearted; He saves those crushed in spirit."

2. **God would demonstrate His power in Paul's weakness.** Sometimes the light of Christ's power shines most brightly against the dark backdrop of our suffering.

2 Corinthians 12:9b-10

Paul didn't just endure his trials and survive his suffering. He found the supernatural strength to "boast" and "take pleasure" in his suffering and weakness.

I don't fully understand why, but God has determined to do some of His most significant work through sickness, pain, and trial. It could be that what the world really needs to see—far more than a miracle or healing—are people who find joy, peace, and trust in God even in the midst of their suffering.

> *How has a "thorn" helped you grow in your faith?*
>
> QUESTION **#3**

> *When have you experienced God's grace during a time of weakness?*
>
> QUESTION **#4**

Roni Bowers, a South American missionary, wrote the following just a few weeks before being killed in a plane crash: "God often chooses to do something different with your life than you envisioned. But it's OK. He's still God, and He still loves you. As long as your confidence in God remains strong in the midst of all the questions and myriad emotions, you will be OK. He is the only one who remains constant, and life is good if you stay in His arms—God's loving arms. You may not understand where He leads, but you will be safe and secure with Him anywhere, even in death."[1]

Does God still heal? Yes. But God doesn't always choose to heal in the way we want Him to. God delivers us in one of three ways:

1. **Sometimes God delivers us out of our pain and suffering.** This can happen through supernatural intervention. God is still in the healing business, and He sometimes demonstrates His great power through healing.

2. **Sometimes God delivers us through the pain and suffering.** This is how God worked in Paul's life. God doesn't take away the sickness, but He gives us the grace to endure it. In the process, He shapes us deeply and manifests His glory so that others see joy, steadfastness, and Jesus in us as we endure.

3. **Sometimes God delivers us unto Himself.** One of the psalmists wrote, "The death of His faithful ones is valuable in the LORD's sight" (Ps. 116:15). We can get so fixated on this life that we forget the beautiful reality of heaven—the life that awaits us.

Our Heavenly Father is good, wise, and in control. He can be trusted.

When sickness comes to stay, what can we do to express God's love without being trite?

QUESTION #5

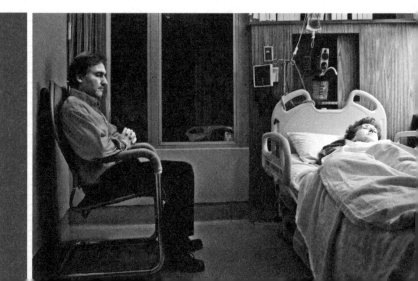

IT IS WELL

Listen to the song "It Is Well with My Soul" and reflect on the reality of God's grace during difficult times. (Using an app to read the QR code below will link to the song on LifeWayWorship.com.)

Use the space provided to record a time when God delivered you through a season of suffering. Do so by writing the story, drawing a picture, making an outline, and so on.

"I think God is nearer to suffering than to happiness. And to find God in this way gives peace and rest and a strong and courageous heart!"

—DIETRICH BONHOEFFER

LIVE IT OUT

Consider the following suggestions for living in the reality of God's all-sufficient grace, even in times of sickness:

▶ **Pray.** Make a list of those you know who are suffering from sickness and disease. Pray boldly for healing each day, and that all parties would find peace in God's will.

▶ **Be there.** Make an effort to engage someone going through a time of suffering. Practice the "ministry of presence."

▶ **Be involved.** Find a tangible way to regularly serve someone going through a time of sickness or suffering. Take meals, offer to babysit, run some errands, or give rides to doctor appointments when needed.

Sometimes illness and disease don't go away. Thankfully, the presence and grace of God don't go away either. Choose to be an avenue of God's grace for someone else.

The Fear of Disease

I have just completed my semiannual CT scan. For nearly 20 years, I've been making this journey to the Scripps Clinic in La Jolla, California. It all began in 1994 when I was diagnosed with non-Hodgkin's lymphoma at the Mayo Clinic in Rochester, Minn. I arranged to receive chemotherapy at Scripps, nearer my home. With each passing year, the staff there has risen higher on my list of heroes.

To continue reading "The Fear of Disease" from *Mature Living* magazine, visit *BibleStudiesforLife.com/articles.*

My group's prayer requests

....

....

....

....

....

....

....

....

....

....

....

....

My thoughts

1. "Remembering and Celebrating an Exceptional Life: Memorial Service for Roni and Charity Bowers," Available at *RockValleyBibleChurch.org/ResourceLibrary/Bowers/Bowers.htm*, [accessed and cited June 13, 2014].

SESSION 4

READY WHEN SEX DESTROYS

Who do you sometimes catch yourself imitating?

QUESTION **#1**

#BSFLlove

> *Influence others to walk in Christ's love rather than in impurity.*

THE BIBLE MEETS LIFE

I've got a friend who once played professional baseball. In a moment of transparent conversation, he shared with me some of his journey.

"When I began playing baseball, I got a real buzz from the crowd," he said. "I started pursuing sexual relationships with women in different cities where we played. My life revolved around these sexual encounters. But one day I woke up and felt numb. I'd left a tiny piece of my soul with each of those women—something I can never get back. I'm tormented by guilt, and I don't know how to have a real relationship. I'm asking God to heal me."

My friend would acknowledge that nothing in his lifestyle was worth imitating. Sadly, people of all ages have a desire to mirror what they see in celebrity culture—including a lifestyle marked by immorality.

The Book of Ephesians points us to Someone who is worth imitating. When we seek to imitate Christ, we discover a life of purity. We discover that we can experience purity, and that we can walk with others to help lead them away from a destructive lifestyle.

WHAT DOES THE BIBLE SAY?

Ephesians 5:1-10 *(HCSB)*

1 Therefore, be imitators of God, as dearly loved children.

2 And walk in love, as the Messiah also loved us and gave Himself for us, a sacrificial and fragrant offering to God.

3 But sexual immorality and any impurity or greed should not even be heard of among you, as is proper for saints.

4 Coarse and foolish talking or crude joking are not suitable, but rather giving thanks.

5 For know and recognize this: Every sexually immoral or impure or greedy person, who is an idolater, does not have an inheritance in the kingdom of the Messiah and of God.

6 Let no one deceive you with empty arguments, for God's wrath is coming on the disobedient because of these things.

7 Therefore, do not become their partners.

8 For you were once darkness, but now you are light in the Lord. Walk as children of light—

9 for the fruit of the light results in all goodness, righteousness, and truth—

10 discerning what is pleasing to the Lord.

Key Words

Fragrant offering (v. 2)—An offering that God accepts or that pleases Him, as first expressed in God's response to Noah's post-flood sacrifice (Gen. 8:21).

Sexual immorality (v. 3)—Taken from the Greek word *porneia* (English *pornography* is related), it refers to sexual relations outside of marriage.

Coarse and foolish talking (v. 4)—Words that are vulgar or dirty, and words that are a silly waste of time.

Ephesians 5:1-4

Paul calls Christ followers to live counter-culturally as citizens of a different kingdom. Christians have experienced the transforming power of the gospel and possess new life in Christ. Therefore, that new life should result in a new walk and a new lifestyle.

Specifically, this is a lifestyle of love. We're to "walk in love, as the Messiah also loved us." Christ's love is our standard for living. That means we should become like Him in all areas of life. **We are to love others in the way He loves us.**

This standard of love applies to sexuality, as well.

God designed sex to provide physical pleasure, for procreation, for relational intimacy, and to be a spiritual object lesson of Christ and the church. God wants us to enjoy deep love and great sex—at the right time, with the right person, and in the right relationship. But sex outside of God's design ultimately leads to shame and destruction. That's why Paul gives us such a strong warning in Ephesians 5.

Notice there should not even be a *hint* of sexual immorality (v. 5). Sexual immorality should never be taken lightly. Paul called us to put up strong guardrails. The path of devastation for many people began with a single visit to one inappropriate website, one inappropriate conversation with a coworker, or one inappropriate message to an old friend on Facebook.

Paul also wrote about our language and conversation, because what comes out of our mouths reveals what's in our hearts. We are not to engage in "coarse … talking," which literally means "shameless talk." Paul also prohibited "foolish talking." The word *foolish* comes from the Greek from which we get our word *moron*. We should not engage in stupid, moronic talk. And we shouldn't engage in "crude joking." This is about vulgar and inappropriate joking and innuendo.

These kinds of behaviors and talking "are not suitable" at any time for those who are called to walk in love and light.

> *Why do we minimize certain sins and give greater attention to others, such as sexual sin?*
>
> QUESTION #2

Ephesians 5:5-6

Paul underscored the seriousness of sexual immorality by talking about God's judgment on sin. A life of impurity and immorality will have consequences.

Verses 5-6 are not referring to the Christian who gives in to temptation or falls into sexual sin during a weak moment. Rather, Paul is describing people who are unredeemed and habitually immoral, impure, or greedy. Paul wrote something similar in 1 Corinthians 6:9-10, where he gave a broader list of habitual sins that keep people from inheriting the kingdom of God. But he immediately followed up in verse 11 by offering great hope through these words: "And some of you used to be like this."

Many of us could give testimony that we *used to be* adulterers, thieves, greedy, dishonest, or sexually immoral. No matter your past, the truth is that all of us were once captive to sin—but the transforming power of the gospel has set us free and broken the bondage to sin. Praise God for His grace!

Still, God's grace doesn't give us a free pass to sin. He doesn't turn His head and look the other way. In fact, Titus 2:11-12 says it is grace that teaches us to say "no" to all ungodliness and worldly passion and "yes" to living righteous, upright lives. God is serious about sin because it's an affront to His holy nature, and He knows how much it will harm us and keep us from the good life He wants to give us.

That's why Paul told us not to be deceived (v. 6). As a pastor, I deal with people all the time who've been deceived when it comes to sex. They thought a secret affair was what they needed to make them happy, but it ended up destroying their families. They thought looking occasionally at pornography wouldn't hurt them, but they ended up addicted. God's standards never go out of style or get outdated. They are always in our best interest. And when people violate God's standards, they invite God's judgment.

In what ways does impurity deceive us?

QUESTION #3

Ephesians 5:7-10

Paul urged us to the high and holy calling of purity. That means we don't think like the world thinks or watch what the world watches. We don't view sex the same way they do. Why? "For you were once darkness, but now you are light in the Lord" (v. 8). No two things could be more opposite than darkness and light.

Verse 9 helps us get a picture of what it means to walk in light by focusing on goodness, righteousness, and truth. "Goodness" has to do with personal character; it's love in action. "Righteousness" is seen in our fairness, justice, and care for others. "Truth" includes practicing integrity; it involves honesty, purity, and wholeness.

So how do we help someone who isn't living according to God's standards of sexuality? Consider the following:

1. **Don't have a self-righteous attitude.** Your sin may not be exactly the same as another person's, but *all* of us are sinners. As you seek to minister to someone caught in sin, do so with a keen awareness of your own sinfulness.

2. **Love unconditionally.** A relationship grounded in love earns us the right to speak into someone else's life. Show your love by your actions and speak it with your words.

3. **Pray and look for the right opportunity.** Ask God to soften your heart, soften the other person's heart, and provide the right opportunity to talk.

4. **Honestly but gently share God's standards and desires.** Show how God has established His standards of purity for our own good—because He loves us.

5. **Follow up.** Send an email, write a note, or make a call to let the person know you want to help.

> *How do we determine whether our actions are aimed at pleasing ourselves or pleasing God?*
>
> **QUESTION #4**

> *What can we do to encourage each other to live pure lives?*
>
> **QUESTION #5**

DARKNESS AND LIGHT

Use the space provided to list ways you've seen darkness and light exemplified in today's culture with regard to human sexuality.

DARKNESS

The use of sex as a marketing strategy.

....

....

....

....

....

....

....

LIGHT

The fight against human trafficking.

....

....

....

....

....

....

....

"Sex is considered both a sacred act between two people united by God and the best way to sell suntan lotion."

—MARY PIPHER

LIVE IT OUT

How can you apply these verses in your own life? Consider the following suggestions for avoiding impurity:

▶ **Evaluate your words and actions.** Where do you see evidence of sexual immorality in what you say and do?

▶ **Memorize Ephesians 5:3.** Hide God's Word in your heart as an internal reminder to strive for purity.

▶ **Talk about it.** It takes courage to go against the grain on issues like sexuality—but courage is needed in our culture. As you have opportunities, share your personal convictions and commitments about sexual purity with others. Be bold.

Like my friend, we've all made mistakes in the realm of sexual immorality. Maybe you feel like you've gone too far to come back—but you haven't. Trust me, you can still be a model for sexual purity. You can choose to be someone others will want to imitate.

Continuing Education

God doesn't consider sex to be taboo. In fact, sex was God's idea. He created us male and female, and He instituted marriage with the intent that two would become "one flesh" (Genesis 2:24).

Why then, do so many couples fail to find mutual satisfaction in this important area of marriage?

To continue reading "Continuing Education" from *HomeLife* magazine, visit *BibleStudiesforLife.com/articles*.

My group's prayer requests

....

....

....

....

....

....

....

....

....

....

My thoughts

SESSION 5

READY WHEN HOMOSEXUALITY DEVASTATES

What were some of the most memorable rules in your family?

QUESTION *#1*

#BSFLnewlife

Share the hope and new life all can have in Christ.

THE BIBLE MEETS LIFE

Few people are happy with rules. As kids, and even as adults, we often balk at rules because they feel restrictive. They keep us from doing what we want to do.

Unfortunately, many look at God's rules in the same way. Popular culture has rejected God's rules for lifestyle issues as out-of-date ideas that hamper progress. *If God loves me, He surely wouldn't keep me from doing what I want to do and living like I want to live. After all, He created me this way, right?*

Our culture has become most vocal with this faulty thinking on the issue of homosexuality.

The Bible shows us that God's rules—His commands for how to live—are for our benefit. The commands in Scripture are not arbitrary; they were given to help us. God has instructed us out of His love for us. The same principle applies to what God says about homosexuality. Let's consider what the Bible teaches on this subject and how we can respond with truth and love.

WHAT DOES THE BIBLE SAY?

Romans 1:18-27; 1 Corinthians 6:9-11 (HCSB)

Rom. 1:18 For God's wrath is revealed from heaven against all godlessness and unrighteousness of people who by their unrighteousness suppress the truth, **19** since what can be known about God is evident among them, because God has shown it to them. **20** For His invisible attributes, that is, His eternal power and divine nature, have been clearly seen since the creation of the world, being understood through what He has made. As a result, people are without excuse. **21** For though they knew God, they did not glorify Him as God or show gratitude. Instead, their thinking became nonsense, and their senseless minds were darkened. **22** Claiming to be wise, they became fools **23** and exchanged the glory of the immortal God for images resembling mortal man, birds, four-footed animals, and reptiles.

24 Therefore God delivered them over in the cravings of their hearts to sexual impurity, so that their bodies were degraded among themselves. **25** They exchanged the truth of God for a lie, and worshiped and served something created instead of the Creator, who is praised forever. Amen. **26** This is why God delivered them over to degrading passions. For even their females exchanged natural sexual relations for unnatural ones. **27** The males in the same way also left natural relations with females and were inflamed in their lust for one another. Males committed shameless acts with males and received in their own persons the appropriate penalty of their error.

1 Cor. 6:9 Don't you know that the unrighteous will not inherit God's kingdom? Do not be deceived: No sexually immoral people, idolaters, adulterers, or anyone practicing homosexuality, **10** no thieves, greedy people, drunkards, verbally abusive people, or swindlers will inherit God's kingdom. **11** And some of you used to be like this. But you were washed, you were sanctified, you were justified in the name of the Lord Jesus Christ and by the Spirit of our God.

Key Words

Delivered them over (Rom. 1:24)—God turned people over to the consequences of their sin. He loosed restrictions on those consequences so people felt the brunt of their actions.

Sanctified (1 Cor. 6:11)—When people come to faith in Christ, they are set apart by the Spirit to live in holiness before God. Without salvation, holiness is impossible.

Justified (1 Cor. 6:11)—Believers receive a new standing before God as sinners who have been declared righteous, not on their own but sharing in Christ's righteousness.

Romans 1:18-23

Sometimes we have to see the mess we're in before we can appreciate the grace God has extended to us. That's why verse 18 begins with words that are hard to hear: "God's wrath is revealed from heaven" (v. 18). Basically, Paul delivered the bad news before he gave us the good news.

We like to focus on God's grace, kindness, and compassion. Certainly, all of that is true of God, but it's not the complete picture of His character. Let's be honest: some things make God angry. The Bible uses the word "wrath" to describe God's reaction to those things.

What had angered God in these verses? We can summarize it in one word: sin. God hates evil and will display His wrath toward sin. Unlike human anger, God's anger is not self-centered. Rather, God gets angry because sin always ends in self-destruction—God is rightfully angry. He is a holy God, and sin is an affront to Him.

Our sin is rebellion against God, but we don't rebel out of ignorance. Romans 1:19-20 teaches that God has made Himself known to all people. A billboard never exists for itself; it points to something else. God has provided a cosmic billboard called "creation" that's been designed for one purpose: to point us to Him and His glory.

Although God has made Himself known through His creation, many have rejected the knowledge of God and chased after their own foolish and destructive desires. "For though they knew God, they did not glorify Him as God or show gratitude" (v. 21).

By declaring they "knew God," Paul wasn't saying such people have a relationship with Him. Rather, they are aware of God—they have what we might call "head knowledge" of Him. By choosing not to glorify or give thanks to God, however, they reject His truth about Himself. Such rejection is followed by a clear path of rebellion that includes futile (worthless) thinking, moral insensitivity (darkened hearts), and idol worship.

> *How does the reality of a Creator influence our discussion of sexuality?*
>
> QUESTION #2

Romans 1:24-27

God will not force people to follow Him. That's why Paul declared that "God delivered them over in the cravings of their hearts" (v. 24). The phrase "delivered them over" means abandoned or surrendered. In other words, God surrendered the people to let them follow their own rebellious paths and sinful desires.

Homosexuality is one of those sinful desires. Paul spoke plainly and specifically about it, and so can we. Verses 26–27 give us a clear and unequivocal teaching on the consequences of deviating from God's design concerning sexuality. Paul wrote these words while living in Corinth, where a brothel often shared space with a temple. Idols were on every corner. Some religious practices included the use of both male and female prostitutes. Virtually all moral rules had been thrown out. No boundaries. Sexual sin is evidence of rebellion against God's design for all life; it's rejection of the design—and the Designer—at the center of creation. Paul wrote with those conditions in mind.

Paul made the case that when people lose their wonder for God and reject Him and His creative design, God gives them up to their own ways. And those ways have devastating consequences.

I understand that reading an indictment like this feels harsh in today's culture of absolute tolerance. But it's like going to the airport. Security agents scan our luggage in order to protect all travelers from anybody or anything dangerous. They look into our stuff—they challenge our "baggage"—and they do it to protect us.

In the same way, the Lord points at certain things and says: "That's dangerous. It's not in your best interest. You need to remove it or it will hurt you." That's what's happening in Romans 1. God points His finger at several sins—including homosexuality—and says, "That's dangerous; it will hurt you." How does it hurt? Sin mars the image of Christ in us; it deprives us of the family God intended; and, if we remain unrepentant, it places us under God's wrath.

> *What emotions do you experience when you contemplate the topic of homosexuality?*

QUESTION #3

1 Corinthians 6:9-11

What are the similarities and differences between the behaviors listed in verse 9 and 10?

QUESTION #4

In these verses, Paul candidly confronted those who had certain habitual practices from which they were unwilling to repent and gave evidence they would not enter the kingdom of God. Paul wasn't speaking about people who have occasional moral failures. Instead, this passage refers to people who—by their habitual sinful practices—say to God, "I don't want any part of You."

Notice that homosexuality is only one of the issues on the list. As you read the sinful actions described in verses 9-10, think about the sins that once defined your life. Every sin on Paul's list is equally destructive. Each of them will harm you and bring destruction to you. Each will crush your soul, alienate you from God, and bring death into your relationships and into your body.

As followers of Jesus, we can't ignore that God condemns the practice of homosexuality. But it's just as important to recognize God no more condemns practicing homosexuals than He does those who lust with their eyes or are greedy in their consumption. God is equally concerned with each sin listed in this passage.

Verse 11 reminds us there is hope for all in Christ. How do we reflect that hope to people impacted by homosexuality?

QUESTION #5

Therefore, we must treat the act of homosexuality as we do other temptations and sins. We need to be forthright and truthful as we present the truth of the Scriptures, but we must do so with humility and compassion—not with a sense of condemnation or superiority.

Paul didn't leave us with condemnation. He gave us a powerful source of hope in verse 11: "And some of you used to be like this. But you were washed, you were sanctified, you were justified in the name of the Lord Jesus Christ and by the Spirit of our God."

At the moment we place our faith in Christ, we're changed and made righteous before God. That's the beauty and the power of the gospel.

WHAT WOULD YOU SAY?

Based on Scripture, how would you respond if a friend or family member made the following statements regarding the practice of homosexuality? Choose one.

"I can't help the way God made me. If He didn't want me to act on these desires, He wouldn't have created me this way."

....

....

"Homosexuality is not a moral or religious issue. It's a civil-rights issue."

....

....

"I'm gay and I want to follow Jesus. What should I do next?"

....

....

LIVE IT OUT

How will you respond to the truths explored in this passage? Consider the following options:

▶ **Reject hate.** Ask the Holy Spirit to highlight and remove any judgmental or unloving attitudes you may have developed toward those who practice homosexuality.

▶ **Seek knowledge.** Research books, articles, or podcasts to learn more about the biblical approach to homosexuality.

▶ **Build relationships.** It's hard to love those we don't know. Seek to make positive connections with gay individuals in your spheres of influence. Look for opportunities to show Christ's love and proclaim His truth.

There will always be rules, and there will always be those who dislike them. God's rules and standards have not changed, but neither has His love. Choose to be a channel of His truth and love.

Morality in First-Century Rome

Morality in first-century Rome and the Roman Empire reflected the plurality of cultures from the Latin west and the Greek east. Within that geographical expanse and the diverse moral cultures of the empire, the Christian gospel providentially appeared and succeeded: "When the fullness of the time came, God sent forth His Son" (Gal. 4:4, NASB).

To continue reading "Morality in First-Century Rome" from *Biblical Illustrator* magazine, *visit BibleStudiesforLife.com/articles.*

My group's prayer requests

....

....

....

....

....

....

....

....

....

....

My thoughts

SESSION 6

READY WHEN PORNOGRAPHY CONTROLS

What's good and bad about a secret?

THE BIBLE MEETS LIFE

Some secrets are fun—like knowing about a surprise party, knowing the best place to fish, and knowing the secret to an illusion. Other secrets are anything but fun. For example, the number one secret in America is who views pornography on the Internet.

▶ 13 percent of all web searches are related to erotic content.

▶ Almost 9 out of 10 young men (85 percent) and almost half of young women (48 percent) report viewing pornography.[1]

We don't like talking about pornography, but it's not limited to the secular world. Another terrible secret is that 50 percent of Christian men and 20 percent of Christian women regularly view pornography.

So what does the Bible have to say about this tsunami of sexual content that's washing over our communities? Sexual temptation and immorality were major issues in the early church, which is why the apostle Paul had much to say about sexual purity.

WHAT DOES THE BIBLE SAY?

1 Thessalonians 4:3-8 (HCSB)

3 For this is God's will, your sanctification: that you abstain from sexual immorality,

4 so that each of you knows how to control his own body in sanctification and honor,

5 not with lustful desires, like the Gentiles who don't know God.

6 This means one must not transgress against and defraud his brother in this matter, because the Lord is an avenger of all these offenses, as we also previously told and warned you.

7 For God has not called us to impurity but to sanctification.

8 Therefore, the person who rejects this does not reject man, but God, who also gives you His Holy Spirit.

1 Thessalonians 4:3

According to Paul, it's God's will for us to be sanctified. That's why verses 3-6 record three ways we can be sanctified, or "set apart":

▶ Avoid sexual immorality.

▶ Practice self-control.

▶ Don't take advantage of others.

The root word for immorality in Greek is *porneia*. This was a broad word that referred to all sorts of sexual distortion: adultery, fornication, homosexuality, and all behaviors associated with those sins—including sexual fantasies and lust.

All such practices are prohibited by God and are morally wrong.

Avoiding sexual immorality requires resolve and diligence, especially in today's world. Even if you don't go looking for sexual content, it's likely to come looking for you.

▶ Seven out of ten youths have accidentally come across pornography online.

▶ Nearly 80 percent of unwanted exposure to pornography takes place in the home.[2]

Want to help others avoid sexual immorality? Lead the way. No responsible parent would ever drop their young children off to wander the streets of downtown Los Angeles. Yet, parents often allow kids to wander the streets of the Internet without any restrictions or supervision. That's asking for trouble in today's world.

Talk often and openly with your loved ones about the dangers of pornography. Have clear expectations and rules for the electronic devices your family members use. To help others avoid sexual immorality, we must be engaged, purposeful, and tenacious.

> *What are some root causes that make pornography so prevalent in our society?*
>
> **QUESTION #2**

1 Thessalonians 4:4-5

In verse 4, Paul wrote that everyone should learn "how to control his own body" (and its desires). By doing so, we can avoid *porneia* of all kinds—including pornography. Through the power of the Holy Spirit, we can learn to control our sexual urges. We're not victims of our sexual urges and impulses. We can control our bodies "in sanctification and honor."

A major component of self-control is "pre-deciding." As much as you seek to avoid sexual temptation and put up healthy guardrails in your life, sexual temptation will still cross your path. It's inevitable. But you can't wait until that moment to decide your response. Commit to do what's right before you're tempted. Make the decision up front about what you will do—and not do—to avoid temptation. The more specific you can be in your "pre-decisions," the more helpful they will be when temptation does come your way.

Specifically, make pre-decisions about what you'll watch, what you'll read, where you'll go, and with whom you'll be alone. For example, part of controlling our bodies is controlling what we allow our eyes to see. And part of self-discipline is controlling what websites we visit and what channels we watch by controlling what buttons we allow our fingers to push on the remote control.

Paul contrasted the self-disciplined life of a believer to the pagans who live according to their "lustful desires." Unfortunately, in our culture we often see little difference between the sexual values and practices of believers and unbelievers. As followers of Jesus, we ought to be distinguishable in our culture by the way we put up healthy and righteous guardrails to protect ourselves from falling into temptation.

Why is the battleground of the mind so important?

QUESTION #3

1 Thessalonians 4:6-8

Whenever a person engages in sexual sin, it doesn't just impact him or her. Like shrapnel, the effects of sexual immorality will damage and wound those around us.

When Paul wrote, "One must not transgress against and defraud his brother in this matter" (v. 6), he was talking about sexual immorality. When we commit sexual sin, we end up wrong and taking advantage of everyone involved. Sexual sin never occurs with a nameless object. Pornography is more than "just images," because those images are of somebody who was created in the image of God—somebody for whom Jesus died. Pornography is exploitation.

Together, these verses contain a strong, straightforward warning. When we engage in pornography and other sexual sin:

> We invite God's judgment and discipline into our lives.

> We are living contrary to our new nature and calling as followers of Christ.

> We are rejecting God Himself.

Since these commands to sexual purity came directly from God, they are timeless. **No matter how much culture shifts and changes, the call to sexual purity remains the same.**

This teaching can seem harsh and narrow-minded unless you understand why God would be so adamant about steering us away from sexual immorality. God is not anti-sex. He gives us strong prohibitions against *porneia* because He knows how He designed us. He knows that within marriage, sex is a wonderful gift of intimacy, pleasure, and love. But when sex is experienced outside the bonds of marriage, it creates all kinds of problems and consequences. Because He loves us and wants to protect us, God has put up high fences for our sexual purity.

What is your initial reaction to the references to God in this passage?

QUESTION #4

How can we help a family member or friend who is struggling with pornography?

QUESTION #5

THE RIPPLE EFFECT

The use of pornography doesn't just impact individuals. Use the chart below to detail the consequences of pornography throughout the different levels of society.

Individual

....

Family

....

Local church

....

Local community

....

Culture

....

The body of Christ

....

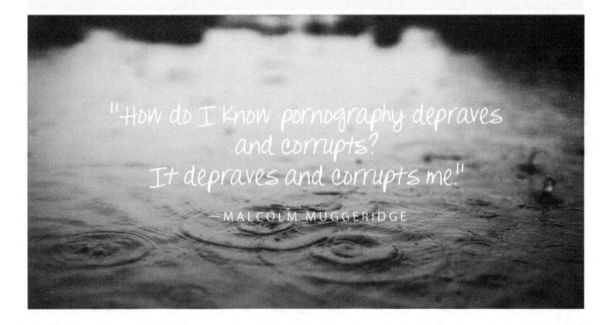

"How do I know pornography depraves
and corrupts?
It depraves and corrupts me."

—MALCOLM MUGGERIDGE

LIVE IT OUT

What steps will you take to fight sexual temptation? Consider the following suggestions:

▶ **Develop clear convictions.** You will never drift into sexual purity. Make a commitment now to reject *porneia* in all forms.

▶ **Get software.** There are many forms of accountability. To reject pornography, the first step is installing accountability software on your computers and other devices.

▶ **Offer help.** If you know people caught in the trap of pornography, help them get the resources they need to overcome. This may include personal accountability, counseling, or joining a support group.

It's no secret there's great value and benefit in maintaining purity, even when no one is around—*especially* when no one is around. The choice is yours. Be someone who practices purity.

Excerpt: The Resolution for Men

When God created sex for a man and his wife alone to enjoy, He permanently linked its pleasure to marriage, love, intimacy, and lifelong commitment. Each of these keeps the sexual relationship meaningful and reinforces a couple's union in marriage. In holy matrimony, sexual pleasure is grounded in love, freely shared, and maintains its priceless meaning and many healthy benefits. There is no cost. No shame. No guilt. No regrets.

To continue reading this excerpt from *The Resolution for Men*, by Alex and Stephen Kendrick, visit *BibleStudiesforLife.com/articles*.

My group's prayer requests

....

....

....

....

....

....

....

....

....

....

....

My thoughts

1. "Pornography Statistics" (2014 edition), [cited 13 May 2014]. Available from the Internet: www.covenanteyes.com.
2. Ibid.

Ready: Ministering Life to Those in Crisis

As followers of Jesus, we need to be the people others look to for help. We don't have to know all the answers, but we can point to the One who is the answer. Let's be ready as the hands and feet of Jesus.

Christ

Jesus didn't live in isolation from others, simply waiting for His time on the cross. Jesus lived among people—loving them and ministering to them. Jesus has placed His Holy Spirit in our lives, and He desires to minister to people through us.

Community

The church is a place for broken people. Even as believers, we need to experience help and ministry from others. God wants believers to love, serve, minister, and be a conduit of His grace to one another (see 1 Pet. 4:8-11).

Culture

The problems, challenges, or sins of other people are never an invitation to judge them. Rather, the issues they are facing are opportunities for us to minister the love and grace of Christ. When we step in to help, encourage, or minister, we point to the One who is the ultimate help they need.

GENERAL INSTRUCTIONS

In order to make the most of this study and to ensure a richer group experience, it's recommended that all group participants read through the teaching and discussion content in full before each group meeting. As a leader, it is also a good idea for you to be familiar with this content and prepared to summarize it for your group members as you move through the material each week.

Each session of the Bible study is made up of three sections:

1. THE BIBLE MEETS LIFE.

An introduction to the theme of the session and its connection to everyday life, along with a brief overview of the primary Scripture text. This section also includes an icebreaker question or activity.

2. WHAT DOES THE BIBLE SAY?

This comprises the bulk of each session and includes the primary Scripture text along with explanations for key words and ideas within that text. This section also includes most of the content designed to produce and maintain discussion within the group.

3. LIVE IT OUT.

The final section focuses on application, using bulleted summary statements to answer the question, *So what?* As the leader, be prepared to challenge the group to apply what they learned during the discussion by transforming it into action throughout the week.

For group leaders, the *Ready* Leader Guide contains several features and tools designed to help you lead participants through the material provided.

QUESTION 1—ICEBREAKER

These opening questions and/or activities are designed to help participants transition into the study and begin engaging the primary themes to be discussed. Be sure everyone has a chance to speak, but maintain a low-pressure environment.

DISCUSSION QUESTIONS

Each "What Does the Bible Say?" section features at least four questions designed to spark discussion and interaction within your group. These questions encourage critical thinking, so be sure to allow a period of silence for participants to process the question and form an answer.

The *Ready* Leader Guide also contains follow-up questions and optional activities that may be helpful to your group, if time permits.

DVD CONTENT

Each video features Chip Ingram teaching about the primary themes found in the session. We recommend that you show this video in one of three places: (1) At the beginning of group time, (2) After the icebreaker, or (3) After a quick review and/or summary of "What Does the Bible Say?" A video summary is included as well. You may choose to use this summary as background preparation to help you guide the group.

The Leader Guide contains additional questions to help unpack the video and transition into the discussion. For a digital Leader Guide with commentary, see the "Leader Tools" folder on the DVD-ROM in your Leader Kit.

For helps on how to use *Bible Studies for Life*, tips on how to better lead groups, or additional ideas for leading, visit: **www.ministrygrid.com/web/BibleStudiesforLife.**

The Point: God calls us to defend those who can't defend themselves.

The Passage: Exodus 23:1-3,6-9

The Setting: After freeing the children of Israel from Egyptian slavery and delivering them safely across the Red Sea, God established a covenant with them for them to be His special possession (Ex. 19) and presented them with the Ten Commandments (Ex. 20). For the next several chapters, including these verses from Exodus 23, God continued to lay out His expectations and guidelines for His people.

QUESTION 1: What examples of injustice cause your blood to boil?

> *Optional activity:* Bring donuts or another snack for this week's meeting. Before group members arrive, hide half the snacks. Offer the food to group members as they arrive. When you run out, apologize for failing to bring enough. Once everyone arrives, bring out the remaining snacks and serve those who went unfed. Point out that you've demonstrated injustice on a small scale. If time allows, ask group members to discuss how they felt when some people received food and others didn't.

Video Summary: In his opening message, Chip talks about how we're to minister to people who are suffering from injustice. In Exodus 23, God shows us what it looks like to do life with one another. He clearly communicates that we're not to deny injustice. Micah 6:8 says, "He has told you what is good and what it is the LORD requires of you: to act justly, to love faithfulness, and to walk humbly with your God." Reflecting His character and what He requires of us means standing up for people who can't stand up for themselves.

WATCH THE DVD SEGMENT FOR SESSION 1, THEN USE THE FOLLOWING QUESTIONS AND DISCUSSION POINTS TO TRANSITION INTO THE STUDY.

- In his message, Chip shared an experience he had with injustice and how he responded. What injustice have you witnessed that burdened your heart?

- Chip's burden led him to seek out opportunities to confront injustice beyond the situation he witnessed. What might be the next step for you? How can you make a greater difference?

WHAT DOES THE BIBLE SAY?

ASK FOR A VOLUNTEER TO READ ALOUD EXODUS 23:1-3,6-9.
Response: What's your initial reaction to these verses?

- What do you like about the text?

- What questions do you have about these verses?

TURN THE GROUP'S ATTENTION TO EXODUS 23:1-3.
QUESTION 2: Why are we sometimes tempted to blend in with the crowd?

This question is intended to give group members an opportunity to examine the reasons it may be easier to identify themselves with the majority rather than step out and stand up for something that may not be popular or accepted. This should be a general question for group discussion—not yet connected to the issue of abortion.

> *Optional follow-up:* How would you define the concept of justice?

MOVE TO EXODUS 23:6-7.

QUESTION 3: How does this passage influence your response to issues such as abortion?

Use this question as an opportunity for group members to actively verbalize their specific response to abortion and other examples of injustice thru the lens of Exodus 23:6-7. Encourage them to talk about what they can and will do about the issue beyond simply avoiding abortion in their own lives.

> **Optional follow-up:** Who are the innocent and defenseless in our community?

CONTINUE WITH EXODUS 23:8-9.

QUESTION 4: How does justice in this passage compare with the "justice" we typically see?

This application question gives group members an opportunity to compare how Scripture defines justice with how our society typically defines and carries out justice. You might also guide them to consider what our definition of justice—whether God's or society's—communicates about what's important to us.

> **Optional activity:** Direct group members to complete the activity "Finding Value" on page 11. If time permits, encourage them to share their responses.

QUESTION 5: What behaviors can we adopt or change in order to defend those who can't defend themselves?

This question is designed to move group members toward life application and to start them thinking about how, specifically, they can make a difference in the lives of those who experience injustice. Through developing a plan of action they'll be required to identify things they need to start doing as well as things they can do differently.

> **Optional follow-up:** When have you truly seen justice done?

Note: The following question does not appear in the group member book. Use it in your group discussion as time allows.

QUESTION 6: How do your experiences as an outsider affect how you treat others?

This question will give group members an opportunity to examine how their own personal experiences color the way they view injustice as well as how those experiences have changed the way they treat victims of injustice.

LIVE IT OUT

Encourage group members to consider these three things they can do this week to address the pain of wrong decisions and defend the lives of others:

- **Pray.** Pray each day for the thousands of unborn babies currently at risk. Pray for the women and families who have been impacted by abortion.

- **Get involved.** Consider writing letters to your congressional representative and other elected officials on this vital issue.

- **Give what you can.** Contribute to a local crisis-pregnancy center. Donate money or volunteer your time to help in this important work.

Challenge: We've all had those moments when we've marveled at a blatant lack of justice. Sometimes the issues seem so great that we can't imagine how we could ever make a difference. Other issues often seem to go unnoticed. But our God is a God of justice and He calls us, His people, to practice justice. This week, look for opportunities to step in and be a voice for someone who is voiceless.

Pray: Ask for prayer requests and ask group members to pray for the different request as intercessors. As the leader, close this time by committing the members of your group to the Lord and ask Him to give each of you courage to step up when someone needs a champion for justice.

SESSION TWO: READY TO HELP THE POOR

The Point: Demonstrate God's heart for the poor.

The Passage: Deuteronomy 15:7-11

The Setting: Frightened by the report of giants in the land of Canaan, God's people chose to remain in the wilderness rather than enter the promised land intended for them. The wandering years had now passed, and Moses' tenure leading the people was about to expire. But prior to his exiting the scene, Moses reviewed for the people all the instruction the Lord had thus far given them.

QUESTION 1: What would you have a hard time living without?

> *Optional activity:* Money is something everyone has a hard time living without, especially in today's culture. As an object lesson, pass a $50 or $100 bill around the group. Ask group members to contemplate their emotional reactions when they receive the currency as well as when they give it away.

Video Summary: This week Chip talks about generosity as a posture of life. We can give without being generous. And that stems from the fact that our definition of generosity is often different from that of God. Wherever our money goes, our hearts follow. If we give to those who truly need it, with open hands and hearts, our hearts can't help but change. And that's how we need to give if we want to show His love to those in need.

WATCH THE DVD SEGMENT FOR SESSION 2, THEN USE THE FOLLOWING QUESTIONS AND DISCUSSION POINTS TO TRANSITION INTO THE STUDY.

- In his message Chip shared, "God wants us to give our access, not our excess." In what ways does this statement change the way you have defined generosity?

- What are some ways you can work to cultivate a heart of generosity? Be specific.

WHAT DOES THE BIBLE SAY?

ASK FOR A VOLUNTEER TO READ ALOUD DEUTERONOMY 15:7-11.
Response: What's your initial reaction to these verses?

- What questions do you have about these verses?

- What do you hope to gain from studying about how you can best respond to people in need?

TURN THE GROUP'S ATTENTION TO DEUTERONOMY 15:7-9.
QUESTION 2: What do you think of when you hear the word "generosity"?

Encourage group members to give their immediate reactions—this is the rare moment where you'd prefer they not stop and think before joining the conversation.

> *Optional follow-up:* What is your first response when you see someone standing in a public place asking for money?

QUESTION 3: How is generosity toward the poor both a heart issue and a hand issue?

This question draws directly from the words of Moses in verses 7-9. It also provides group members with an opportunity to sort out for themselves the interaction between the attitude and the action, the belief and the behavior.

> *Optional activity:* Direct group members to complete the activity "Heart and Hand" on page 20. If time permits, encourage volunteers to share one action they can take to combat poverty in their community through generosity.

CONTINUE WITH DEUTERONOMY 15:10-11.

QUESTION 4: What factors should we consider when seeking to help the poor?

The answers group members give for this question will provide a perfect lead-in to the optional follow-up question. Remind group members that every situation is different, and encourage them to be aware of ways they can discern how the poor can be best helped considering their circumstances.

> *Optional follow-up:* In addition to giving money, what are other ways to help the poor?

QUESTION 5: How does this passage challenge us to be fully engaged in ministry to the poor?

You may wish to filter all discussion for this question through the broader lens of Deuteronomy 15:7-11 and James 5:1-6.

> *Optional follow-up:* Both of these passages illustrate excuses for not helping the poor. What excuses do you need to reject when it comes to helping those in need?

Note: The following question does not appear in the group member book. Use it in your group discussion as time allows.

QUESTION 6: How would you describe the line between being stingy and being a good steward?

To answer this question, group members have to define for themselves what it means to be stingy and what it means to be truly generous. Their answers will also help them identify any faulty thinking they may still be holding onto.

LIVE IT OUT

How can you change in light of these truths from God's Word? Invite group members to consider these practical ideas for serving the poor:

- **Remove the blinders.** Make an effort in the coming days to seek out the poor and underprivileged in your community. Consider looking where you don't typically look and going where you don't typically go.

- **Plan to give.** Set up your budget to include a monthly amount for giving when you encounter spontaneous needs.

- **Get involved.** Find a local ministry your church supports that helps the poor, the orphans, or the needy. Choose to become an active contributor.

Challenge: When we direct our money and time to the poor, our hearts, attitudes, and actions toward them tend to change as well. As you actively seek opportunities to serve the poor, take time to write down ways you observe these changes happening in your own heart and life. These notes will provide you with tangible reminders of how God blesses us when we take the time and effort to demonstrate the very heart of God to those who need it most.

Pray: Ask for prayer requests and ask group members to pray for the different requests as intercessors. As the leader, close this time by committing the members of your group to the Lord. Ask God to fill each person in your group with a passion for generosity. Ask for specific opportunities to serve the poor in the days to come—and for the courage to take advantage of those opportunities whenever possible.

SESSION THREE: READY WHEN SICKNESS COMES TO STAY

The Point: God's grace is sufficient—even in times of sickness.

The Passage: 2 Corinthians 4:16-18; 12:7b-10

The Setting: Believers of the first century experienced the same physical challenges and trials that the general population did, but their distinct minority status subjected them to additional trials through discrimination and/or persecution. Yet Paul stressed whatever difficulty one endured would only be momentary when measured against the promise of eternity with Christ. He used a personal example of his own "thorn" to emphasize God's grace and ability to demonstrate His strength despite our difficulties.

QUESTION 1: When you're sick, what helps you feel better?

Encourage group members to share a part of their stories by asking this follow-up question: "When was the last time you experienced that relief?"

> *Optional activity:* Bring a can of chicken noodle soup to the group gathering as an example of something that makes people feel better when they're sick—or bring a cup of instant soup as a gift for each group member. If you have the time and facilities to make it work, consider serving a cup of soup to each group member during the opening portion of the discussion.

Video Summary: In his video message this week, Chip talks about how we can be messengers of hope when sickness won't go away. It's a difficult situation to be in—both for the person experiencing illness and for the loved one who has been called by God to bring perspective, to walk alongside the sick. "We are pressured in every way but not crushed; we are perplexed but not in despair; we are persecuted but not abandoned; we are struck down but not destroyed. … Therefore we do not give up. Even though our outer person is being destroyed, our inner person is being renewed day by day" (2 Corinthians 4:8-9,16). We trust in Him to help us deliver this truth.

WATCH THE DVD SEGMENT FOR SESSION 3, THEN USE THE FOLLOWING QUESTIONS AND DISCUSSION POINTS TO TRANSITION INTO THE STUDY.

- Who is that person you need to help focus on what is not seen?
- What steps will you take this week to help that person see that God isn't done with him or her yet? How can you begin to communicate hope in the midst of a situation that may seem hopeless?

WHAT DOES THE BIBLE SAY?

ASK FOR A VOLUNTEER TO READ ALOUD 2 CORINTHIANS 4:16-18; 12:7B-10.
Response: What's your initial reaction to these verses?

- What questions do you have about these verses?
- What new application do you hope to get from this passage?

TURN THE GROUP'S ATTENTION TO 2 CORINTHIANS 4:16-18.
QUESTION 2: What are some questions people ask as they deal with health-related issues?

This question is impersonal in that it doesn't require group members to talk about their own health-related questions. However, don't stop them from answering from their personal experience if they choose to do so.

Optional follow-up: How does focusing on the eternal help us endure the temporary?

MOVE TO 2 CORINTHIANS 12:7B-9A.
QUESTION 3: How has a "thorn" helped you grow in your faith?

This question provides group members with an opportunity to share a personal story while also allowing them to identify spiritual markers from their own journey of faith.

Optional follow-up: How do you handle it when a prayer isn't answered as you hoped?

CONTINUE WITH 2 CORINTHIANS 12:9B-10.
QUESTION 4: When have you experienced God's grace during a time of weakness?

This is another opportunity for group members to share a personal experience with the group. Being asked to process how God's grace has impacted them in their own weakness with also help them be more aware of how they can in turn help others in similar situations.

Optional follow-up: In what ways have you experienced strength when you felt weak (v. 10)?

QUESTION 5: When sickness comes to stay, what can we do to express God's love without being trite?

This question is designed to give group members an opportunity to brainstorm specific ways they can minister on the deepest levels to people experiencing extended illness. Encourage them to listen closely as others share.

Optional activity: Direct group members to complete the activity "It Is Well" on page 31. If time allows, ask for volunteers to share their responses.

Note: The following question does not appear in the group member book. Use it in your group discussion as time allows.

QUESTION 6: What does it require of us to minister to those with long-term sickness?

It's obvious that this aspect of ministry is not for the faint of heart. It requires courage and strength. It's emotional and even scary at times. Allow group members to acknowledge their fears and concerns but help them not to get stuck there. Encourage them to consider also the privileges and blessings that can come from such a call.

LIVE IT OUT

Encourage group members to consider the following suggestions for ways they can live in the reality of God's all-sufficient grace, even in times of sickness:

- **Pray.** Make a list of those you know who are suffering from sickness and disease. Pray boldly for healing each day, and that all parties would find peace in God's will.

- **Be there.** Make an effort to engage someone going through a time of suffering. Practice the "ministry of presence."

- **Be involved.** Find a tangible way to regularly serve someone going through a time of sickness or suffering. Take meals, offer to babysit, run some errands, or give rides to doctor appointments when needed.

Challenge: Have you dealt with the effects of long-term health issues personally or in the life of someone close to you? If so, consider the ways others have reached out to you. What was most helpful? If you haven't experienced illness on this level, talk to people who have. Ask them what actions have helped them most. Use these reminders this week to guide you in knowing how you can best minister to those dealing with illness in their own lives or the life of someone they hold dear.

Pray: Ask for prayer requests and ask group members to pray for the different requests as intercessors. As the leader, close this time by asking the Lord to give you and the members of your group the strength to echo Paul's confidence that His grace is sufficient and His strength is made perfect in weakness.

SESSION FOUR: READY WHEN SEX DESTROYS

The Point: Influence others to walk in Christ's love rather than in impurity.

The Passage: Ephesians 5:1-10

The Setting: Paul went to Ephesus on both his second and third missionary journeys, ministering there three years the second time. Despite his relatively long stay in Ephesus, Christianity faced serious challenges from other religions and philosophies of the day. He wrote this letter to once again lay out the basics of the faith and to reestablish the believers in the truths and lifestyle of life in Christ, regardless of the prevailing social norms around them.

QUESTION 1: Who do you sometimes catch yourself imitating?

Optional activity: It's common for people to imitate celebrities in today's culture. Lead your group in an experiment by bringing photographs of several different celebrities to the group gathering—you can cut these photos out of magazines or print them yourself. During the gathering, hold up each photo like a flash card and ask group members to identify the person and why people might want to imitate him or her. Note: Be sure to choose celebrity photos that are unlikely to be offensive or cause any unwanted disruptions during the group meeting.

Video Summary: This week Chip takes on the topic of sexual purity and addresses our call to live pure lives as well as our responsibility to help others do the same. God wants to use us as instruments in the lives and hearts of others to make sexual purity their norm. Sex matters; and sex is meant to be pure. It binds hearts and souls. It's sacred. But many people today are experiencing sex with shame and baggage, sex without the beauty and intent of God's design.

WATCH THE DVD SEGMENT FOR SESSION 4, THEN USE THE FOLLOWING QUESTIONS AND DISCUSSION POINTS TO TRANSITION INTO THE STUDY.

- Chip talks about how sex outside of God's intent can destroy relationships—with God, with ourselves, and with others. How have you seen this to be true?

- After hearing Chip's message, in what ways do you now feel better equipped to influence the lives of others for sexual purity?

WHAT DOES THE BIBLE SAY?

ASK FOR A VOLUNTEER TO READ ALOUD EPHESIANS 5:1-10.

Response: What's your initial reaction to these verses?

- What do you like about the text?

- What new application do you hope to receive about God's desire for us to live a lifestyle of purity?

TURN THE GROUP'S ATTENTION TO EPHESIANS 5:1-4.

QUESTION 2: Why do we minimize certain sins and give greater attention to others, such as sexual sin?

This question will lead group members to examine how we tend to view sin—individually or as a whole, as a behavior or as a lifestyle—preparing them to unpack this concept in more detail through later questions. As an example, call attention to Paul's mention of greed in verse 3.

Optional follow-up: What are the marks of a life that imitates God?

MOVE TO EPHESIANS 5:5-6.

QUESTION 3: In what ways does impurity deceive us?

The final paragraph on page 39 of the group member book includes pastoral comments from the author that may be helpful as a way of sparking discussion for this question.

Optional follow-up: How do people typically rationalize their sin?

CONTINUE WITH EPHESIANS 5:7-10.

QUESTION 4: How do we determine whether our actions are aimed at pleasing ourselves or pleasing God?

This interpretation question will guide group members to ask themselves whether their actions line up most closely with worldly standards or God's standard of goodness, righteousness, and truth (v. 9).

Optional activity: Direct group members to complete the activity "Darkness and Light" on page 41. As time allows, invite volunteers to share ways they have seen darkness and light exemplified in today's culture.

QUESTION 5: What can we do to encourage each other to live pure lives?

Discussion of this question should begin with the relationships in your group and then move outward to include family, friends, and so on.

Optional follow-up: What is it about your experience of walking in darkness and in light that makes you want to walk in the light?

Note: The following question does not appear in the group member book. Use it in your group discussion as time allows.

QUESTION 6: What factors make you most hopeful about the potential for a renewed dedication to sexual purity in future generations?

Use this question to help group members focus on the difference they can make in the lives of future generations by allowing God to use them to help others stop the cycle of sexual impurity and make God's intent for sex their norm.

LIVE IT OUT

How can you apply these verses in your own lives? Encourage group members to consider the following suggestions for avoiding impurity:

- **Evaluate your words and actions.** Where do you see evidence of sexual immorality in what you say and do?
- **Memorize Ephesians 5:3.** Hide God's Word in your heart as an internal reminder to strive for purity.
- **Talk about it.** It takes courage to go against the grain on issues like sexuality—but courage is needed in our culture. As you have opportunities, share your personal convictions and commitments about sexual purity with others. Be bold.

Challenge: We've all made mistakes in the realm of sexual immorality. You may feel you've gone too far to come back—but you haven't. No matter the misstep, you can still be a model for sexual purity. Commit your life to purity and choose today to be someone others will want to imitate.

Pray: Ask for prayer requests and ask group members to pray for the different requests as intercessors. As the leader, close this time by asking the Lord to grant each of you a fervent desire to live as a model of purity in a world where impurity is the norm.

SESSION FIVE: READY WHEN HOMOSEXUALITY DEVASTATES

The Point: Share the hope and new life all can have in Christ.

The Passage: Romans 1:18-27; 1 Corinthians 6:9-11

The Setting: Romans is Paul's most theological work. His focus is on the gospel as the power of God for salvation and righteousness. But before people will receive salvation, they must first recognize that their sinfulness leaves them in need of salvation. These verses from Romans emphasize the sinfulness of all Gentiles. Additionally, Paul's letter to the troubled church in Corinth reminds them of their personal sinfulness prior to the washing they received in Christ.

QUESTION 1: What were some of the most memorable rules in your family?

To encourage group members to share their stories, ask the follow-up question: "What was your usual reaction to that rule?"

> *Optional activity:* To continue with the theme of rules and standards, bring rule books from different board games to the group meeting. Pass the rule books around the group as an object lesson on the necessity of rules and boundaries in life. If you have time, encourage group members to share stories of when they attempted to break or enforce the rules from their favorite games.

Video Summary: This week Chip talks about a subject that we all recognize to be controversial and emotionally charged—homosexuality. How can we be ready to respond? As believers, God calls us to maintain a balance between love and truth. We are to love and accept individuals involved in homosexuality just as we would love anyone else, but at the same time we're called to speak truth and set boundaries. In many ways this is a sin not so different from many others, but it requires that we be educated and know how to respond.

WATCH THE DVD SEGMENT FOR SESSION 5, THEN USE THE FOLLOWING QUESTIONS AND DISCUSSION POINTS TO TRANSITION INTO THE STUDY.

- On a scale of 1 to 10, how prepared are you to respond to homosexuality in a healthy, helpful way? Explain.

- What concerns or fears do you have about being able to lovingly minister to those who are struggling with homosexuality?

WHAT DOES THE BIBLE SAY?

ASK FOR A VOLUNTEER TO READ ALOUD ROMANS 1:18-27; 1 CORINTHIANS 6:9-11.

Response: What's your initial reaction to these verses?

- What questions do you have about these verses?

- What new application do you hope to get from this passage?

TURN THE GROUP'S ATTENTION TO ROMANS 1:18-23.

QUESTION 2: How does the reality of a Creator influence our discussion of sexuality?

This question is designed to guide group members to the true intention of any discussion of sexuality—the reality of a Creator who loves us and wants only the best for us. The very One who created sex as a gift that is sacred and pure, with very specific intentions. This discussion will reinforce their understanding of who God is.

Optional follow-up: How does God's wrath relate to God's love?

MOVE TO ROMANS 1:24-27.

QUESTION 3: What emotions do you experience when you contemplate the topic of homosexuality?

Remind group members that engaging this question is not an opportunity to abuse or disparage homosexual individuals. This is an opportunity for them to honestly identify any biases or preconceived views that could prevent them from being effect ministers.

Optional follow-up: What factors have changed our culture's view of homosexuality in recent years?

CONTINUE WITH 1 CORINTHIANS 6:9-11.

QUESTION 4: What are the similarities and differences between the behaviors listed in verses 9 and 10?

Look at these verses closely as a group to engage this question at the most effective level. This may mean reading and re-reading, circling words, or examining the commentary found on the DVD-ROM.

Optional follow-up: Explain in your own words the promise you find in 1 Corinthians 6:9-11.

QUESTION 5: Verse 11 reminds us there is hope for all in Christ. How do we reflect that hope to people impacted by homosexuality?

This question will help ensure that group members have an adequate understanding of the text as well as give them an opportunity to apply it to specific situations.

> ***Optional activity:*** Direct group members to complete the activity "What Would You Say?" on page 51 as a way of privately applying the truth of God's Word.

Note: The following question does not appear in the group member book. Use it in your group discussion as time allows.

QUESTION 6: How can we respond with love, grace, and truth to people who experience homosexual desires?

Group members should continue the discussion from question 5 but on a more personal, practical level. Encourage them to be specific as well as truthful about any concerns that still remain. The more honestly they engage, the more prepared they will be to minister when the need arises.

LIVE IT OUT

How can you respond to the truths explored in this passage? Invite group members to consider the following options:

- **Reject hate.** Ask the Holy Spirit to highlight and remove any judgmental or unloving attitudes you may have developed toward those who practice homosexuality.

- **Seek knowledge.** Research books, articles, or podcasts to learn more about the biblical approach to homosexuality.

- **Build relationships.** It's hard to love those we don't know. Seek to make positive connections with gay individuals in your spheres of influence. Look for opportunities to show Christ's love and proclaim His truth.

Challenge: Spend time in Romans 1:24-27 this week. When you find yourself tempted toward tolerance rather than speaking the truth in love, remember that when people lose their wonder for God and reject Him and His creative design, God gives them up to their own ways. And those ways have devastating consequences. Is it more important to avoid a potentially awkward situation and protect yourself or do you truly want the best for others?

Pray: Ask for prayer requests and ask group members to pray for the different requests as intercessors. As the leader, close this time by asking that His Spirit empower each of you to serve as witnesses for God's love and the truth of God's Word, both in your church and in your community.

SESSION SIX: READY WHEN PORNOGRAPHY CONTROLS

The Point: Help others to practice purity.

The Passage: 1 Thessalonians 4:3-8

The Setting: Paul had established the church in Thessalonica during his second missionary journey. While some Jews received his message, many did not. Some of the latter incited a mob, accused Paul of acting against Caesar, and sought to drive him out of town. They even followed him to Berea and stirred up trouble there. Out of concern for the believers in Thessalonica, Paul wrote to encourage them in the faith, including in the ethics of the faith in chapters 4–5.

QUESTION 1: What's good and bad about a secret?

> **Optional activity:** Most forms of sexual sin, including pornography, thrive in the darkness of private thought and private action. Therefore, give your group members an object lesson on darkness by turning out the lights as you discuss Question 1. When you turn the lights back on, remind group members that we all need to shine the light of God's Word on the areas of our lives still shrouded in darkness.

Video Summary: In this last session Chip talks about how we can be ready to make a difference in the lives of those who struggle with pornography. Pornography corrupts and destroys. The problem is big, but there is hope. And we need to be ready to step up and make a difference, helping those who are struggling to break free to learn how to connect with God, restore their souls, and transform their relationships. *Note:* In this session Chip references a video message on parenting and technology that he and his son Ryan created. It can be found at *http://livingontheedge.org/parentingandtechnology.*

WATCH THE DVD SEGMENT FOR SESSION 6, THEN USE THE FOLLOWING QUESTIONS AND DISCUSSION POINTS TO TRANSITION INTO THE STUDY.

- What are some ways we can step up and help someone struggling with pornography to understand how this issue undermines and destroys sacred sexuality?

- How can we best support and encourage without causing shame?

WHAT DOES THE BIBLE SAY?

ASK FOR A VOLUNTEER TO READ ALOUD 1 THESSALONIANS 4:3-8.
Response: What's your initial reaction to these verses?

- What questions do you have about how you can best support those struggling with pornography?

- What new application do you hope to get from this passage?

TURN THE GROUP'S ATTENTION TO 1 THESSALONIANS 4:3.
QUESTION 2: What are some root causes that make pornography so prevalent in our society?

Encourage group members to engage the root causes connected with human nature as well as those connected with technology and increased availability of pornography in modern culture.

> *Optional follow-up:* What's the connection between sanctification and abstaining from sexual immorality?

MOVE TO 1 THESSALONIANS 4:4-5.
QUESTION 3: Why is the battleground of the mind so important?

This question will give group members an opportunity to discuss the power of our thought lives and acknowledge that when the battle isn't fought and won on this level, the sin usually goes further. Consider pulling in Philippians 4:8 as a part of this discussion.

> *Optional follow-up:* What are some things you have "pre-decided" that guide your behavior?

> *Optional activity:* Direct group members to complete the activity "The Ripple Effect" on page 61. If time allows, encourage volunteers to share their responses.

CONTINUE WITH 1 THESSALONIANS 4:6-8.

QUESTION 4: What is your initial reaction to the references to God in this passage?

Encourage group members to examine the text closely. This question will require them to personally interpret who God is based on 1 Thessalonians 4:6-8.

> *Optional follow-up:* What reasons are given in these verses for avoiding all sexual immorality?

QUESTION 5: How can we help a family member or friend who is struggling with pornography?

This question is designed to help group members leave your session with a plan of action, but it should be approached as hypothetical. Don't ask for or allow group members to name specific individuals struggling with an addiction to pornography.

> *Optional follow-up:* How can we help friends and family members avoid the snare of pornography?

Note: The following question does not appear in the group member book. Use it in your group discussion as time allows.

QUESTION 6: How can we address the broader damage pornography causes in our society?

Ending your group time with an application question should leave group members with a sense of action. Encourage them to be specific in answering. Because this question is broad in scope, be prepared to start the discussion with some ideas of your own.

LIVE IT OUT

Encourage group members to consider the following steps they can take to fight sexual temptation:

- **Develop clear convictions.** You will never drift into sexual purity. Make a commitment now to reject porneia in all forms.
- **Get software.** There are many forms of accountability. To reject pornography, the first step is installing accountability software on your computers and other devices.
- **Offer help.** If you know people caught in the trap of pornography, help them get the resources they need to overcome. This may include personal accountability, counseling, or joining a support group.

Challenge: There's great value and benefit in maintaining purity, even when no one is around—*especially* when no one is around. The Live it Out section highlights the importance of actions such as conviction, accountability, and support. Spend some time this week being deliberate about these things. Put a plan in place that will not only help you and your family stay on track but also equip you to help others do the same.

Pray: As the leader, close this final session of *Ready* in prayer. Ask the Lord to help each of you as you move forward to maintain an awareness of how you can best love, support, and minister to people who are fighting against sexual temptation. Ask God to bless the members of your congregation with a strong desire for purity.

Note: If you haven't discussed it earlier, decide as a group whether or not you plan to continue to meet together and, if so, what Bible study options you would like to pursue. Visit *LifeWay.com/smallgroups* for help, or if you would like more studies like this one, visit *biblestudiesforlife.com/smallgroups*.

BIBLE STUDIES FOR LIFE ™

WHERE THE BIBLE MEETS LIFE

Bible Studies for Life™ will help you know Christ, live in community, and impact the world around you. If you enjoyed this study, be sure and check out these other available titles.* Six sessions each.

Pressure Points *by Chip Henderson*

When Relationships Collide *by Ron Edmondson*

Do Over: Experience New Life in Christ *by Ben Mandrell*

Honest to God: Real Questions People Ask *by Robert Jeffress*

Let Hope In *by Pete Wilson*

Productive: Finding Joy in What We Do *by Ronnie and Nick Floyd*

Connected: My Life in the Church *by Thom S. Rainer*

Resilient Faith: Standing Strong in the Midst of Suffering *by Mary Jo Sharp*

Beyond Belief: Exploring the Character of God *by Freddy Cardoza*

Overcome: Living Beyond Your Circumstances *by Alex Himaya*

Storm Shelter: God's Embrace in the Psalms *by Philip Nation*

Ready: Ministering to Those in Crisis *by Chip Ingram*

If your group meets regularly, you might consider Bible Studies for Life as an ongoing series. Available for your entire church—kids, students, and adults—it's a format that will be a more affordable option over time. And you can jump in anytime. For more information, visit **biblestudiesforlife.com**.

biblestudiesforlife.com/smallgroups
800.458.2772 | LifeWay Christian Stores

Additional titles will continue to be released every three months. Visit website for more information.